Insanity

Dedicated to all the brilliant people who are promoting reasonable and civilized conversation in the world.

Ari Airio

Insanity

Publisher: BoD – Books on Demand, Helsinki, Finland
Print: BoD – Books on Demand, Norderstedt, Germany
ISBN: 978-952-80-0726-5

I was gradually coming back to reality when I realized that all this is only happening inside our heads. There are some things happening out there also, and in the heads of the others as well, but our perception of those things is severely delusional. Someone else could see pink as black and hear all the sounds completely different than us, but if all the time the same way, we could never understand how fundamentally different our experiences of the world were. Even our own experience varies over time and in different situations; our favorite music and food usually changes with age and the same face might in different states of mind look either appealing or repulsive to us, same make-up either stylish or grotesque. Some animals see infra-red light, use echolocation and sense the earth's magnetic field or other animals' electric fields. Their experience differs so fundamentally from ours that we can't even begin to understand it. And even if we forget the limits of our senses and how they are constantly deceiving us, we are still prisoners of language; how differently we may understand the value and meaning of things. And it's not even a matter of taste but rather the illusion that our brain creates of the world. In our own reality we all have great taste and reasonable opinions.

Different levels of consciousness are like layers of lenses through which our worldview reflects. Deeper levels are limiting the way we can see things on the more superficial levels and the more conflict there is between different layers, the more unclear the image gets. That image starts forming already before our birth and the things that affect us the most are the things that happen to us when we are so young that we can´t really understand them, process them intellectually, or even remember them afterwards. They affect straight to the core that we can´t really get our hands on later in life and everything else is built around it. And since we can´t get our hands on in, we experience it as ourselves. But our personalities only exist as our reactions to our surroundings, there is no us unrelated to everything else. Every moment we react to our environment based on our earlier experiences and we stack new layers, through which we see the world and ourselves, on that core. That is why we might react to our environment in a completely different way than someone else despite growing up in similar circumstances; the way we react to things that are happening to us is way more important than the actual things themselves. And the way we react to them is based on our state of mind, which depends on the previous thing that happened to us, as well as on our reactions to everything else that has ever happened to us.

The deeper the layer which we form delusional opinions on, the harder it is to later change them, because we have been building on them so much beliefs that would just crumble if we would admit that the base assumptions behind them were wrong. Hence a relatively small incident could at its worst distort all our experiences afterwards and grow into enormous proportions. Our most powerful experiences and the feelings related to them sink so deep into our subconscious that whenever they rise back to the surface, they take us, in both good and bad, back to the same state we were in when they were born. This is how passions, traumas and obsessions are born, and everything that we can´t handle emotionally and process intellectually, becomes part of our personality. Every once in a while, some kind of strong experience, like falling in love or the death of a loved one, is able to penetrate those deeper layers and fundamentally changes our perspective on life. But usually those beliefs are not in our conscious mind, or at least we are not questioning them in any way. They are the absolute truths that any reasonable person should understand, even though we can´t necessarily rationalize them in any way. They can be tied to so strong emotions, that we rather die than face and question them, and even trying can cause panic attacks, dissociation, psychosis and crippling depression, or all of those in different combinations.

Opinions are just thoughts tied to emotions. Generalizations lead from generalizations. That´s why our brain stops us from thinking too much or too unpleasant thoughts and keeps up a little optimistic illusion about ourselves and the world, so we would keep on trying and living and trying to live, and foremost passing on our genes. Our selfish genes who are willing to sacrifice us, as long as they can keep on living with the next generation. Most of the time we are on the level of consciousness that differs very little from other animals, and we don´t necessarily leave that level even once in our whole lifetime. On that level there is mainly happening the observation of the end results of different thought processes but not too much anything that could be called actual thinking. We see things from our own perspective and interpret the world in a way that fits into our previous assumptions of it, our thinking is serving our will instead of being able to truly question it. What we think of as ourselves is however just a collection of different conditioned reactions, behavior patterns and prejudices, deep down we are all just big babies experiencing fear or love. If we are able to, even momentarily, free ourselves from everything that we think we are and what we believe in, we can create ourselves endlessly again and little by little get closer to true freedom. The final step of evolution is not biological but spiritual.

Deeper levels of consciousness demand the ability to withstand extreme emotions and drastically different states of mind, but they are not just different emotional states. We can experience the same emotions on all levels on consciousness, but the higher levels also include the kind of freedom of thought that can be extremely difficult to handle. When we go to a deeper level, all the options on the more superficial levels are freed as equal, since they no more have emotional meaning to us. We can put pineapple on pizza if we may, gays can get married and it's allowed to wear socks with sandals. None of those things really matter compared to the fact that all our loved ones are one day going to die, as are we all. Someone might, although, kill their offspring rather than let them marry the wrong person, and honor killings are a prime example of how mental health problems are passed on through religion and culture.

In the deeper levels of consciousness, we see how our opinions and wants are formed for the more superficial levels; we kind of get to take a peek into our subconscious. Because there are more options and less made-up truths, we also get more complete misses. If we go deep enough, we might forget things like gravity, direction of time, existence of different languages, who we are and other limiting factors that usually rule out some options. Our logic functions like in a dream-like state and we return to the same level of imagination that we had as a child, yet we still possess all the information that we have of the world and we try to rearrange our worldview again based on that information. If we are not aware of our condition and just hold on to the first thing that comes to mind, we might think that we are Santa Claus or Napoleon or that we are able to read minds, at least we forget so many norms of behavior and everyday routines that we seem to have completely lost our minds. The down-side of going insane is that it makes it really difficult to act rationally. Pure genius is total insanity.

When we encounter enough things that are in conflict with our fundamental beliefs, we start getting conflicting signals from the levels where those beliefs are located and the harder we hang on to those beliefs, the bigger the conflicts get and the stronger symptoms they bring about. We understand things on the superficial level but on the deeper level we are unable to let go. Or we hang on to something that we deep down already know not to be true. Those conflicts between the different levels of consciousness are the taproot of our problems and we are going to have to face them sooner or later, whether we are willing or not. Usually not, a terrifyingly large proportion of us would rather give themselves electric shocks than sit quietly for 15 minutes with just their own thoughts.

If we hang on for too long to something that we already deep down know to be false, and there are plenty of those since our subconscious is constantly rearranging things, we have to constantly lie to ourselves more and more. Just like when we tell a little white lie and are forced to cover it up with new lies that get more and more ridiculous. The bigger that inner lie gets to grow, the stronger feelings are tied to it and when it finally breaks up to the surface, we are forced into a level of consciousness where we are unable to understand reality anymore. All the possible and impossible possibilities feel equally plausible and we just pick one that we desperately cling on to. At the same time our brain might also rearrange the way we interpret our sensory input and we can see, hear and feel things that other people can´t. But inside our heads, where everything is happening anyway, those things are completely real.

 Too accurate perception of the reality is not too good either. If we understand more than we can handle, we get stuck on a level where we are constantly aware of the injustice of the world, our own mortality and the meaninglessness of it all. Suicide is said to be the only purely rational act and pure rationality should literally be avoided like our life depended on it. Happiness in intelligent people is however not the rarest thing in the world because intelligence makes us unhappy but because unhappiness makes us intelligent. Depression in moderate doses is a perfectly natural and useful part of our lives that helps us to grow. When the egocentric worldview becomes unbearable, it forces us to look at things from a broader spectrum. In essence, depression is narcissistic despair, the inability to accept that the world is not the way we want it to be. Yet depression is not caused by us being selfish, but usually quite on the contrary. Being unselfish makes it even harder to bare the cruelty and injustice of the world and our inner conflicts may lie so deep within ourselves that they are almost impossible to reach, since we are not just suffering for ourselves but for the whole world as well. And because we see only the negative side of things in that state, by trying to think ourselves out of depression, we just keep sinking deeper and deeper.

 Incoherent signals between different levels on consciousness affect different neurotransmitters, through which they cause different kind of psychological and physiological symptoms and the magnitude of those symptoms is directly comparative with how much of our feelings we can handle. And on the other hand, some external factors such as malnutrition or overstraining affect those signals through neurotransmitters. And besides that, our diet affects our mental balance, our mental balance also affects what kind of diet is good for us, since our stomach and brain live in symbiosis.

 Natural athleticism and superintelligence are an almost impossible combination because they both strain the same systems from different directions and demand contradicting qualities. Stress makes us sick and overstaining can even kill us through different illnesses. The deeper we go to our consciousness, the more we are also controlling our vital functions and if we realize something too far out of our capabilities to withstand, without going insane, our body starts a self-destruction mechanism because it can't bare itself anymore. We don't get sick because we are knowingly lazy, and we can't kill ourselves by pure willpower. We don't get depressed or manic because of the things that are in our conscious mind, but because of those that we cannot consciously handle. Understanding evolution and its meaning cost Darwin his physical health. The Will to Power cost Nietzsche also his mind.

 Once we get in balance with ourselves, we can go back to the level of consciousness where we are functional, and that spectrum can also broaden considerably. When we learn how to function on different levels, we can, besides defining ourselves by ourselves instead our surroundings doing so, also move between different levels in a more controlled manner. We can on the other hand see significantly more different options, but at the same time also accept the fact that things are not how we think and would like them to be. Pseudo-intellectual self-help memes offer us an easy solution in not thinking anything unpleasant and leaving all the negative people on their own, but the pursuit of constant happiness is an utterly irrational idea. Besides getting us to break in front of every little misfortune, it also stops our emotional growth and stopping makes us bore to death, unless we are constantly making up some meaningless pastime. Leaving the negative people on their own also makes them even more negative which leads to them getting left out even more and that cycle goes on until they lose their minds or lives. After that we can feel sympathetic for them for the one last time, maybe even post on social media about how important it is to show people that we care before it´s too late, before it´s time to be all happy and positive again, so we don´t get left out ourselves.

Through meditation, fasting and different forms of therapy, we can learn how to face different levels safely and in a controlled manner but that takes time and meeting them in a safe environment doesn't directly help us to function in the world, it just gives us tools that we can try to apply one situation at a time. We can also artificially bring ourselves back to a functional level by using different mind-altering substances, but that leaves out the growth process and genuinely facing ourselves, and the fundamental reasons behind our symptoms remain unattended and get to grow even bigger. This is why pharmaceutical psychiatry has not evolved other than superficially since the times when Freud offered cocaine as a solution to almost everything, nor can it ever really evolve past that, regardless of how well-functioning medicines we would be able to develop. We have to try out different options and combinations of medications because we are using them to treat artificially defined illnesses that tell nothing about the reasons behind the symptoms and those reasons are so complicated that precisely fixing the changes that they are causing is absolutely impossible. Explaining mental health problems just as chemical imbalance of the brain and seeing that imbalance as the cause instead of a consequence means cutting so many corners that it has similar scientific value as astrology. Change in brain chemistry changes only the level of consciousness, the perspective, the level of awareness. But without inner conflict, there is no problem. And where getting the mind in balance also balances the body, medication causes side-effects that at their worst lower our quality of life much more than the original reason that caused us to lose our minds in the first place.

All addictions are fundamentally caused by the same internal conflicts and that's why we get hooked on so different drugs and some of us don't get hooked on anything. With stimulants we get more speed and excitement in our lives and opiates replace our missing feeling of being loved. A heroin addict might live on the street with shit in his pants but still feel like life is going pretty well after getting his fix. Some psychiatric medications cause us to gain a hundred pounds, get diabetes and lose our sexual abilities, and even if we still feel a little bit better in some sense, objectively there really is no reason for that. Numbing with drugs without offering any other treatment is just a chemical version of locking into a basement.

When we are depressed, we are exhausted because our body is signaling us that it would be time to stop and think, and while manic, we go on overdrive because it would be time to act, but in excess they can both turn into vicious self-reinforcing cycles. Then we should be able to somehow turn it around, take action while depressed and stop to think while manic. Anti-depressants can however cause bi-polar disorder, since the reason for our depression still exists, but we are forcing ourselves, with medication, into being functional and we have to overcompensate so the reason wouldn't pop back up to the surface. With downers we run into opposite problems because in both situations we are just dealing with different sides of the same problem. Either we benumb in front of the thing that we don't want to face, or we try to distract ourselves by focusing on everything else and possibly even create an alternative reality where that thing doesn´t exist, and even if it does, we try to fix it completely at one sitting. The same situation can at its worst feel too boring and too exciting at the same time, and we don´t have a clue of the direction that we should even try to get to.

When we find a substance that makes us feel like we are in balance, we are not willing to give it up at any cost. The other option would be learning how to function on those levels of consciousness where our problems are located at, but for some of us those inner conflicts may lay in so deep that it´s practically impossible to get in touch with them and in that case a medication can definitely be in order, and the need for it doesn´t mean that we are weaker or worse in any way, but without therapy and/or self-examination, it does nothing but hide the symptoms. Artificial manipulation of our brain chemistry can also make it significantly harder to genuinely face ourselves and our true feelings, and that´s why medication should always be the last option. Especially permanent medication that is meant to just hide the symptoms and keep us on a functional level. If we are offering it as the first solution, we are just turning the natural crises and misfortunes of life into chronic illnesses, instead of them being possibilities for emotional and spiritual growth and a step towards self-discovery, peace of mind and happiness. The side effects and withdrawal symptoms of the drugs are also easily interpreted as worsening or renewing of our illness and once we are hooked, it can be almost impossible to get off them ever again.

On the contrary, different kind of psychedelics could be a tremendous help when used correctly as therapeutic tools, because they allow us to visit for a short amount of time on the levels where our problems are located. Even though they don't bring anything from outside of ourselves or cure anything by themselves, they can give us completely new perspective on things and a lot to work with. Psychedelic therapy should also be part of the curriculum of anyone studying psychology since it's almost impossible to understand the mind purely theoretically. If we haven't been in psychosis or visited the higher levels on consciousness in some kind of controlled manner, we are completely missing one direction of existence, and even the most important one if our aim is to help someone struggling with their mental health. It's like a person blind from the birth trying to understand colors or a deaf person trying to understand music, that's the closest we can get. If we learn the functions of the mind only from books, we remain dilletantes in psychology and tourists in insanity.

Resetting our brain by getting drunk is based in some sense on the same principle as psychedelics, even though in that case the cure is a lot of times worse than the disease. Psychedelics make us more aware of ourselves, delete predetermined answers and behavior patterns from our minds and let us think more freely. Alcohol on the other hand makes us less aware of ourselves and instead of thinking, we are controlled by those behavior patterns and different instincts. It brings all the monkeys and demons living inside of us to the surface and analyzing our drunk behavior while sober can tell us a lot about ourselves; the amount that our behavior changes while we are drunk is directly relatable to the amount of our inner conflicts. The effect is however completely opposite if we start using alcohol regularly in order to numb our minds and to free ourselves from thinking, when we just stop our emotional growth and possibly even develop an addiction that causes it to downright regress.

 Beside mental problems, psychedelics can also help with different addictions, that usually go hand in hand. Withdrawal is also mostly about withstanding extreme states of mind and that's why it's so hard to hang on to our decision to quit. In addition to the original problem, that we needed medication for, or what caused us to self-medicate and develop an addiction, we have artificially modified our consciousness and because we mainly react to change, taking away anything that makes us feel better causes withdrawal, whether we are aware of it or not. When our existence becomes unbearable, our level on consciousness changes, and if we don't recognize and control it, we are turned on autopilot and we will do anything in order to fulfill our need. Similar kind of emotional abductions happen all the time on a smaller scale in our everyday lives, when we feel like we are acting completely rationally, but afterwards we can't explain our actions, at least if we are honest with ourselves. We eat unhealthy foods, impulsively buy stuff we don´t really need, skip exercise, act selfishly or mean, start smoking again, get wasted or do some other harmful thing despite our earlier decision. We know how we are supposed to act, and we would want to do so, but our egos can rationalize almost anything and make up the most ridiculous excuses, when in reality we have just broken on the level that is not under our control. And it doesn´t even require unbearable physical withdrawals, just slight discomfort and perhaps a little misfortune that makes us feel like a victim and deserving of some kind of compensation. Or perhaps some kind of familiar stimulus, that connects our desire to so strong positive feelings, that we cannot resist it. Happiness is the ability to enjoy withdrawal.

 If we feel like we are forced to give up something and try to change our behavior with sheer willpower, without changing ourselves as well, we are always going to eventually break and go back to our earlier way of acting. As long as we stay the same, we are also going to react to same kind of stimulus the same way. If we still deep down believe that something that is harmful to us is actually fun, we are going to endlessly break into repeating it, regardless of the problems it´s causing to us. We have to precisely change that what we want in order to make true changes and to get closer to inner balance. We get out of the loop by figuring out the answer to the right question, once we figure out the question that already includes the answer.

Staying the same means the stopping of emotional and spiritual growth and that's what becoming an adult means in many ways. We become locked into some fundamental assumptions of life and start interpreting the world in a way that supports those assumptions and usually those assumptions are just publicly approved opinions that we absorb under social pressure. This is why the world starts looking clearer and our confidence grows, because we think the same way as everyone else and, from our own perspective, we become wiser. Almost like continuously playing the same videogame on the same difficulty level. And some of us follow the cultural programming so faithfully that they almost seem like CPU controlled, with only an occasional bug breaking that pattern.

Herd instinct was truly useful when we were still living in the wild and going solo could have also endangered everyone else's life beside our own. But after we had lifted ourselves above nature, many of our natural instincts became mostly harmful to us and are stopping us from making the necessary changes. Culture has developed kind of in the same way as evolution, but there has been somebody lying to somebody else in almost every turn, in order to gain personal gain, and forcing ourselves into believing in those lies is one of the biggest reasons behind our internal conflicts and ill-being. At least the original reasons of our customs have many times already been forgotten or lost their meaning and they have become empty rituals that have, according to our new understanding, become useless and possibly even harmful. The amount of all the existing knowledge is growing so rapidly that we are constantly becoming more and more stupid compared to it. And possibly more stupid in general, since there is, instead of the demand for thinking for ourselves, so much information readily available.

It is by all means important to learn from history so we wouldn't keep repeating the same mistakes over and over again or have to invent the wheel again every time, as well as common codes for behavior are in order to ensure peaceful and functional interaction, but doing anything only because it has been always done, just keeps us prisoners of the past. With age we may learn again to let go and relax, once we figure out that there are no absolute truths, nor do the superficial things mean anything. As just the right amount of senile we might become wise and possibly even truly happy. Or we cling to the truths that were in fashion in our youth and become one of those grumpy seniors who think everything used to be better.

Consciousness itself is like a mirror through which we see ourselves and the consciousness sees itself through us. Consciousness is the idea of all existence and we are all part of the same consciousness, and this doesn't involve only humans but animals as well and even everything abiotic. Plants are naturally aware in a completely different way than we are, and rocks don't have brains to ponder their existence with, but without consciousness we would also be just biological machines and we could live our whole lives on autopilot in a same way as if making coffee, walking, or doing something else where we don´t really have to pay any attention. For animals, and especially for plants, the experience of existence is probably way more intense than for us since they are constantly really in the moment, instead of overanalyzing everything all the time.

 Our brain is constantly processing an incredible amount of information and making decisions based on that information and we are only aware of a tiny fraction of those processes but not actually affecting them in any way. We feel like we are making carefully considered decisions according to our free will, but that´s almost the same kind of an illusion as the sun orbiting the earth. Even any conscious reaction to the realization that there is no free will, is not a sign of free will. Just like becoming aware that we are insane doesn´t make us sane, any more than becoming aware that we are 5´7" makes us 6´2". If we become depressed and get stuck in bed, or become completely reckless, it´s just our inevitable reaction to that realization and occurs according to what kind of person we are based on our previous experiences. Nor does that realization mean that we are not responsible for our actions, we are on the contrary also responsible for all the indirect consequences of our actions, since everyone else is also reacting to them in the only way that they possibly can. There is no sense in pride or shame, we are just either lucky or unlucky to be who we are.

Turning the other cheek is not only wrong towards ourselves, but also towards them who have offended us, because it gives them a signal that their actions have no consequences and feeds their bad behavior. We ought to forgive them, for they don't know what they are doing, but also make sure that they don't keep doing it. We don't have to accept any kind of behavior, and some actions can and should be hated, but hating a person for their actions is like hating water because of floods.

Nevertheless, at some point we inevitably go back to the level where we feel like we are in control. And on that level, we possibly are. In the same way that matter exists, even though everything is fundamentally just energy. We can't walk through walls and we can't not make a decision, because not to make a decision is also a decision. And we can't even not do anything since laying still and doing nothing is still laying still and doing nothing.

Even though our will isn't exactly free, it changes based on how well we are aware of ourselves and our surroundings. On the highest level of consciousness there is no any kind of will whatsoever and free will is a contradictory concept by itself. When we want something, we cease to be free and we can never choose against our will, even if we feel like it. Regardless of how long we struggle with ourselves, we always end up choosing what we want the most, even if we don't understand ourselves and our motives at the time.

The highest level of consciousness is absolute freedom and sheer nonverbal understanding without any thoughts, fears or hopes; pure feeling of connection with the universe and something completely different than our physical being. Consciousness is the idea of everything, the universe watching itself through us, that some of us call God. A human being is half animal and half god, a bit like a Finn is half Russian and half Swedish.

Jesus, Buddha and Mohammed all got into that deepest level and then tried to interpret it to fit their own time and culture. Buddha did the best job by telling that no-one can teach anyone anything. The fundamental meaning of religion is, through educational stories and different kind of paradoxes, to help us give up our everyday state of mind for a while and create a connection to a higher level of consciousness, or at least give us an experience of the existence of one. Taking god into our heart and giving our life to him doesn't mean believing some literal truth, but genuinely listening to our conscience. In the middle of selfishness and selflessness, discipline and hedonism, living in the moment and living for the future, between everything there is a place where we have an experience of being in balance and feel like we are doing the right thing. Not just for ourselves, but for everyone else as well, and not just for that moment, but for all time to come. Without that experience we feel emptiness that we try to desperately fill with superficial pleasures and purely rational explanation of the world and the meaning of it all, and by doing so, we just get even more out of balance. Faith is essential to our well-being, but religion is just a tool, not an end, and interpreting them literally just leads to spiritual death. We read them like the devil reads the bible and search for loopholes, through which we are able to do harm but still follow the rules, and if we believe that anything is forgiven just by repenting, soon there is nothing forbidden anymore. At least we are better people than those who don´t believe in our god and therefore we have the right to treat them as inferiors.

There is still a somewhat right idea behind every religion, even though their literal content is wrong. It´s completely insane to first claim that god is beyond all human understanding and then give him petty and humane features and believe that he has ordered strict rules about our sexuality, clothing and diets. Fundamentalists fighting over those rules are further away from god than most atheists. An extreme Buddhist sounds equally ridiculous as a black white supremacist. In general, all religious leaders have interpreted religious texts from their own limited perspective and then forced their views on everyone else as well, which has turned their meaning upside down and instead of setting us free, they have been used to control and enslave us. This is on the other hand exactly what we want, nothing is as frightening as true freedom because it includes equal responsibility, and meeting god can be such a hard experience to handle that it causes us to seek security from religion.

Religion and science have been in constant battle, even though they are just different sides of the same thing and become one when you look at them close enough. God is the truth and the truth is god, and truth should also be the only goal of science. But where we have religious scientists, who understand that the essence of religion is not in the literal content, we also have scientist who treat science as religion and, regardless of intellectually understanding the scientific method, relate to existing scientific theories emotionally as unchangeable holy truths. Science can never give us those in a same way god is beyond all human understanding and that's a thought that can be really hard to handle. Not all opinions are equal, and science is the only way to get closer to the truth, but there is a tremendous difference between thinking we are less wrong than everyone else or that we are absolutely right. The greatest trick Confirmation Bias ever pulled was convincing us that it didn't exist if we were aware of it.

That's why we cling on to our own worldview, whether it's based on religious texts or latest scientific theories, and we can't approve any contradicting evidence or allow the basis of it to be questioned in any way. We have always attacked against anyone with new groundbreaking theories, criticized their personalities as well as their theories and made a laughing stock out of them, and only the future generations have understood and appreciated their accomplishments. But we have on the other hand adopted some new inventions so eagerly, that we can't stand any kind of critique about them, even though the history of science is full of failed experiences and theories that later turned out to be incorrect.

This kind of attitude is extremely harmful in medicine and other practical applications, that directly affect our wellbeing. Diagnostics is evolving all the time and we are constantly developing new methods to diagnose diseases that we didn´t previously understand, but unfortunately a large portion of doctors relate to medicine as if it was a perfectly formed field of science and even believe that they handle it so perfectly that they deem all patients whose symptoms they can`t explain as lazy or hypochondriacs. Genetically modified organisms we either take as a solution to all our problems with food production, or a ticking timebomb straight from hell. They may be both or neither, but the conversation around them is a prime example of how propping up our own truth becomes more important than finding out the actual truth. It´s a completely different thing to cross-breed plants in a way that they produce the features that we want, or add new genes that could never naturally end up in them. This could be completely harmless or potentially cause problems that we can´t even begin to understand yet, but genetic modification is anyway probably at least as safe as asbestos.

If we dare to even speculate the subject, we are told that without genetic modification even bananas would have so much seeds that they would be unedible, even though genetic modification has nothing to do with it. Increasing food production is nevertheless, right after increasing Monsanto´s profits, the biggest reason for genetic modification and questioning it in any way means that we want people to starve to death, even though nearly half of all the food produced in the world is thrown away and way more people are dying from obesity than malnutrition. Nor are bigger crops helping the starving African children in any way anyway, if their families have been kicked out from their traditional farming grounds, where a Chinese financier is now producing food for export. Neither do the bigger crops help anyone else, if they are result from plants that can endure so much pesticides that we kill all the pollinators as a side result. But thinking any of that is of course heresy, since anything that produces profit in a three-month span is good for the economy and therefore, for the world.

Neoliberal economy policies have, besides replacing religion, also corrupted a large portion of science and especially in economics, which is merely a belief system, the word science is used jolly loosely. It promises us heaven on earth in a form of endless material abundance. We worship money as a god that can solve all our problems as long as we have enough of it. It can of course never do that, but that delusion helps us to keep going day by day in a same way as the promise of an afterlife in never-ending bliss for those who have been doing as they are told.

We say that we would much rather cry in a Mercedes than in a bus and even though that proverb doesn´t make much sense, it reveals something about materialisms relation to happiness and our relation to both of them. Owning a Mercedes doesn´t affect our happiness, but our attitude towards owning it does. And when we have owned it long enough, owning it loses its meaning but losing it hurts just as much, or even more, as getting it gave us pleasure. This is how we get owned by our possessions, even though they only bring us momentary joy. Many lottery winners have spent their winnings in a couple of years and later told that the win spoiled their lives. Some bankers would rather kill themselves and their families than drop into the middleclass after the stock market crash. It´s the same phenomenon as a drug addiction, and the bigger the dose, the harder the withdrawals. And the American Dream is just an empty bubble anyway since capitalism could never bring wealth to all the people of the world.

This is not only because the natural recourses are running low already and the earth couldn´t possibly handle the western standards of living for all the people of the world. The wealth brought about by capitalism has also always been based on exploitation of the underprivileged and the whole system would collapse if we ran out of people to exploit. In western countries we have been able to give up slave labor and give the working-class better living conditions since we have exported a large portion of the physical labor to developing countries where is no minimum wages, work safety, environmental protection nor other extra expenses. Raw materials, food and utility articles are produced with slave- and child labor and the natural recourses of the developing countries are robbed in a ridiculously low price. Twice the amount of the development aid is pumped out of developing countries each year, thus effectively stopping them from developing. There are more slaves in the world than in any other time in history. Regardless of all this, improvement of technology and excessive use of energy, even the western societies are in debt head over heels and on a brink of bankruptcy. Offering even remotely humane living conditions to the poor of the world would cause the house of cards to tumble down and in the same time there are sums going around in the derivatives market, that are so many times bigger than the combined gross domestic product of the whole world, that no-one can even count their precise amount.

We use imaginary money to create more imaginary money, and when cocaine-fueled and adrenaline filled stock brokers can't do it fast enough, we resort to robots that are basically just complicated slot machines. And yet the rising share prices bring no real value to the world, just imbalance. Instead of thinking what we should do, our actions are guided by extreme emotions because we can't relate to money rationally. Monkeys throwing darts make more reliable forecasts about the economy than economists. And then the real world is expected to function in the terms of the casino economy. It's like little children playing Monopoly were forced to cover their losses with real currency out of their pocket money.

In a situation like this, even the neoliberals are crying out for socialism to the rescue, since pure capitalism could never work. Without social security, income redistribution, business support, state build infrastructure and especially bailouts, the system would just collapse and lead to total chaos. As it has done every time deregulation of the economy has gone too far. The second world war could have started without Adolf Hitler but not without the crash of 1929. Some of the scribes have turned it around and claimed that even though the crash was caused by deregulation, it was really caused by not deregulating enough. According to that very same logic, Adolf was an underachiever.

The economy has grown bigger than the people and the system is more than the sum of its parts, anyone inside of it could be replaced and it would mean nothing. It hasn't served our wellbeing for a long time, nor increased our happiness for decades, regardless of the material abundance it has produced. Our part in it, and the most important measure of our worth as human beings, has turned out to be how well we are serving the system. We have transported a large portion of the jobs to offshore, replaced them with technology and laid out huge amount of work-force even from profitable companies in order to maximize profits and now we are blaming people for being unemployed. Instead of distributing the work more equally, we are taking more and more out of the remaining work force, creating conflict between the employed and the unemployed and portraying the unemployed as lazy and despicable parasites, so the employed are easier to blackmail, in fear of getting unemployed, into working with continually worsening conditions.

As unregulated, the system would suck everything into itself, before it would get destroyed, destroying everything else with it. Even now no-one can really control it but some of us are still benefiting from it. The high priests of economy, the little elite, who doesn't understand that they are also going to die with it. The masses are so far staying under control with handouts, but once enough people are unable to fill their basic needs, we shall once again start the search for the guilty. Then the world is going to burn, the streets will flood with blood and leaders are hang on lamp-posts. If all this happens before it's too late, we may still have hope and then we might finally be a little bit readier for socialism.

We should never run out of money and the lack of it should never be an obstacle for anything for it's only a product of our imagination and its value is completely imaginary. What we can afford economically should be completely separated from what we can afford ethically and ecologically. The value of money changes so much that the pay for the same work can be tens of times bigger or smaller in different parts of the word, and in some countries, we could put a child in school for a year with the price of a Happy Meal. The same differences in the value of money that allows us to produce things for richer countries with next to nothing, would also allow us to help the poor of the world with a fraction of the amount that we use for vanities and luxury, but it would turn over some of the benefits that we have gotten out of robbing and oppressing them for centuries. We can´t afford to make ethically and ecologically sustainable choices because we need to constantly pump the maximum amount of profit out of the system.

Money should be an instrument of commerce but when we have enough of it, it becomes an instrument of power. And the one who has most of it, is not going to use that power against his own interests. A certain amount of money reflects the amount that its owner should possess of all the world´s wealth, and even though most of the money is imaginary and has no equivalent in the real world, it can still be used to affect public opinion and political processes in order to make the rules more favorable for ourselves. And in addition to all this, the banks are still manipulating interests illegally, corporations are evading taxes and the rich are hiding their wealth in tax-havens. The game is already rigged and unfair, but in their endless greed they are also cheating in it. Ratings providers are part of the same gang of crooks and charlatans, holding enormous power without any kind of responsibility. Private banks create money out of thin air and besides holding governments as hostages, to be forced to make decisions that benefit the rich if they don´t want the interest rates of their national debts to go up, the changing amount of money is also accelerating both upswings and downturns. The whole monetary system is a pyramid scheme and every time the bubble is burst, there is a redistribution of wealth from the poor to the rich. We are being offered an option in a form of electrically mined money, but as the biggest bubble of them all, it´s not even worth the electricity.

Socialism would be a much more reasonable system than capitalism and that is why it works even worse with humans. All the same products and services could also be produced without constantly pumping money out of the system and, instead of throwaway consumer society, they could be produced according to what is useful and necessary. At least on all the fields whose services are mandatory for people to buy, those services should be produced by the state, since the possible losses are, at least indirectly, anyway collective. For the same reason all the natural monopolies should always be property of the state. They could also be used to practice reasonable employment and social policies and people not needing welfare while working could be taken into account while considering their salaries. The money used for marketing could be used for product development and the products could be designed to last as long as possible instead of breaking as soon after the guarantee ends as possible. Already in the 70s we sent probes to space that are still functioning, but now it seems almost impossible to get a cellphone or a printer that lasts more than two years.

But if socialism is forced upon the people, it causes similar reaction as bringing in democracy from the outside by murdering the dictator. If the culture is not really ready for it, it only leaves a void of power that is filled by the most cruel and ruthless facet possible. This is what happened in Mao´s China and Stalin´s Soviet Union and it led to the deaths of over one hundred million people. Partly because of the paranoid cleansings and partly because both Mao´s great leap forward and Stalin´s five-year plans were completely unrealistic failures and led to the starvation of millions of people. Both systems were in general used, instead of bringing equality and justice for all, as extensions of their leaders' penises and were travesties of the original ideology. Communism does anyhow require a little more surveillance, since it´s not natural for humans to work only for the greater good. But still the human rights in the Soviet Union from the 60s forward where not worse than in the United States during the communist persecutions, which proves that the problem is not the system but the people running it. Soviet Union also won the space race regardless of the moon landing and thus proved that also a communist system can lead to great accomplishments. But at the same time, it was the competition with the west that lead to its downfall. As long as we are competing against each other, we are all going to lose in the end.

The United States was founded on a stolen land after the biggest genocide in history and that was in many ways the climax of the early capitalism. For it always was a merger of political and economic power that used war to ensure and maximize profits. And the United States has honorably and proudly carried on this tradition by being in war or at least meddling with arms into other countries internal affairs for over 220 years out of those some 240 years it has existed. The largest defense budget in the world, that should in all honesty be called offence budget, is also an income redistribution from the taxpayers to the military complex, whose shares a large portion of the most important policymakers are in possession of. War is great business, especially if we take into consideration that it's not only about the amount of natural recourses we get to rob, but also that the people who are collecting the profits are completely different than those paying the costs. With excessive patriotism, continuous asking for god's blessing and praising the military in every possible turn, we can keep up the illusion of fighting for freedom and justice against the forces of evil. When in reality we are fighting in service of the economy that got out of hand, the antichrist, the hydra, the beast of the apocalypse.

All of our evolution has been superficial and the further we go to the right, either economically or politically, the more we should rather talk about degeneration. Unhealthy competition, selfishness and the pursuing of personal gain over others are fundamentally caused by the fear of possibly getting less than somebody else if we are playing fair and everyone else is not. The pursuit of personal gain by every individual is supposed to accumulate to benefit the community, wealth, instead of shit, is supposed to trickle down and the invisible hand is supposed to direct the economy, but reality is obviously something completely different. Co-operation is the only thing that has helped us through hard times and the selfishness of today would not be possible without the social structures we have built together. And even though the increase of our material wellbeing has not increased our emotional wellbeing for decades, we pursue it so blindly that we are willing to sacrifice everything for it, and we are not only competing about who gets to waste the most natural recourses, but also about who gets to waste them the fastest.

 The biggest mistake of the left is to see us as selfless and intelligent beings who are in everyday life able to work for the benefit of a bigger community than our own herd and for the future as well. This is why left-wing intellectuals have so often become estranged from reality, and for the same reason there are no right-wing intellectuals. Socialism works as an ideology and capitalism works in practice and their harmonization is similar kind of endless process as us getting in balance with ourselves. Both sides are right and wrong at the same time and there is no, nor will there ever be, an all-inclusive theory because reality is way too complicated for that. Our brain is the most complicated structure in the universe and in order to create a perfect system, we should somehow be able to connect 7 billion of them in a chain.

Capitalism works as long as it's regulated enough to serve the people instead of the people serving capitalism. Difference in income is useful as long as it rewards from effort but doesn't encorage blind greed. Corporations are useful as long as they produce work and income but are not big enough to use political influence to their own advantage.

Socialism works as an ideal that is useful to aim for, but is not realistic, or even necessary, to actually reach. When we think that we are enlightened, we are just going on an extreme ego trip and when we think we have created the perfect model for society, we take the first step towards totalitarianism. We can make ourselves better only from reality, by taking small steps and seeing where they lead. If we create an ideal in our minds and use it as a measure of how things ought to be, we open the possibilities for so enormous problems that we can't even begin to understand them. Especially if we created that ideal because we can't handle the reality.

One would nevertheless think that we could somehow figure out a better combination of the two, than the one we have now, in which the profits are privatized to benefit the small elite, but losses are socialized. Even to the extent of bankers paying bonuses for themselves, out of the bailout packages paid by the taxpayers, after ruining the world economy. But power and wealth have on the other hand always gone hand in hand in every system and this phenomenon doesn't only involve humans. That, that the one who already has the most, also gains the most, is almost an unavoidable law of nature. One of those that could be useful for us to learn how to control, if we want to finally evolve beyond lobsters and create a culture that is going to benefit us all and not continuously crumble over its own impossibility.

Culture defines how we are supposed to talk, dress, think and act. Where religion decides on our behalf about the spiritual and other deeper issues, culture is in charge of the more superficial things. Differing too much from the norm usually means isolation, different forms of bullying and social exclusion. We dress fashionably, act and think in a way we are supposed to and gather to exchange publicly approved opinions in conversations that don't include anything original and whose meaning is merely to make sounds together in order to strengthen our feeling of togetherness. Taboos make sure that we do not discuss any forbidden subjects, but the strong emotions that they cause indicate that they are precisely what we should talk about. Whether it's drugs, socialism or religion, the reason why we are not allowed to talk about them is that we have been blatantly lied to. But if somebody says something contradicting the public opinion, we only remember them having a different opinion than the majority and therefore being wrong, regardless of if their opinion later became universally accepted truth, since the meaning of those conversations is not to exchange opinions, but to talk by turns, and nobody remembers their actual content. When Socrates tried to bring a little depth into public conversation, he was sentenced to death for corrupting the youth.

Nowadays we usually react to someone differing from the norm by either getting amused or annoyed by them not understanding how we are supposed to be. Unless they are part of a special group that we can categorize, and they act and dress according to that group´s standards. Punkers and hipsters look ridiculous in their own strictly limited ways and the fierce bikers symbolizing freedom actually have way more rules within their own group than the surrounding society. Besides our personality, our clothes are also telling about the group we belong to, and those who don´t seem to belong to any group we see as threats because we can´t define them. It´s easier to cause contempt with toe shoes than with tattoos. Some of us change their style constantly according to what´s the latest fashion and we might think they are superficial because of that, even though the truth might be completely opposite, and they see clothes as something so meaningless that they just buy the ones that are most easily available. Sometimes we have a little bit too serious attitude towards clothing; Cato junior despised Julius Caesar´s red toga so passionately that after Caesar rose to power, he rather killed himself than left himself in the hands of a man with so poor fashion sense.

Traditionally dressing has also been used to indicate our gender and possibly even our sexual orientation. Some of the loudest spokespersons of the sexual minorities are however seeing them as ambiguous social constructs and demand everyone to be treated only as individuals, despite themselves defining 76 different genders and sexual orientations, in order to categorize everyone as efficiently as possible. It´s not in any way relevant if our gender identity or sexual orientation are depended on social, genetic or psychological factors, any more than any other attributes of our personality. Whether there actually is some permanent god given soul that was somehow accidentally born into the wrong body or we just couldn´t emotionally handle not being able to pee standing up as a girl, doesn´t change our experience of it. We are the way we are, for reasons we don´t understand, normal is just an illusion and an average person is approximately as common as a unicorn. Problems are born when we claim that being different is wrong and try to fix it by force, or we completely deny heteronormativity and biological differences of the sexes, because small minorities don´t want to handle the emotions related to them. All men are fundamentally pigs, and all women are crazy, even though all of us are a little bit of both. Homophobia is typically a consequence of suppressed homosexual urges and getting upset by someone else´s sexuality, whether we think it´s too abnormal or too normal, is a relatively good indicator that the problems is inside our own heads.

Sex is anyway the single most overrated and misunderstood thing in the world. Women like it way more than men, but men want it more, leaving both confused and frustrated. Everything being sold with sex and the whole culture being built around of either forbidding or praising it, and many times both at the same time, keeps everyone a little bit paranoid about it. We want it only because we are programmed to do so, but much like everything else, if we can just look at it from the outside, we see it as completely ridiculous. Yet it is the driving force of everything, no matter how complicated the foreplay around it may look.

Through family, nationality, race, favorite sports team, musical taste, political party and sexual orientation we belong simultaneously into different kind and different sized overlapping groups and we define ourselves through group identity, dividing ourselves into us and them. We are essentially just groups of monkeys that usually get along but from time to time get excited to throw feces at each other. As a part of a smaller group, we function inside of that group in a same way as the group functions as a part of a bigger group, but in reality, all of those groups are artificial, and we are all part of the same enormous group in which we should learn to get along. We still need those smaller groups for practical reasons and fusing them to together is not in any way meaningful, just the understanding that them fighting each other is insane and doesn't help anyone.

Our similarities are as imaginary as our differences and how well we get along depends mainly on which ones we are paying attention to. We have just happened to be born in different roles and cultures, but we are fundamentally driven by the same needs and instincts. We are all just trying to find our place in the world, and by working together we could make that place a little bit better for everyone.

Tolerance turns into intolerance once we start tolerating just certain type of tolerance and discrimination is still discrimination, regardless of how positive it may be. If Apu would have been shitting on the streets, raping people and sending texts asking for bobs and vagene, maybe he wouldn't have stood out so much from all the negative stereotypes and would have been left alone. Political correctness is the new totalitarianism.

People are like assholes, everyone has an opinion. Neoliberalism, Neoconservatism and Postmodernism walk into a bar. Knock knock. Who's there? World War III.

We can get along with our neighbor, despite being completely different kind of people and liking very different things, as long as we don't move in together and try to force each other into being exactly like ourselves. In the same way we can respect and understand different values and cultures but trying to mold them together by force leads to constant conflict.

Within our own culture almost anyone of us could be replaced with someone else without too much trouble and it is essential that we fill our own part without thinking too much. In a highly specialized society we have mastered one special skill and earn our living by repeating it daily, but outside of our own field our worldview is very limited and superficial. Controlled by our culture and surroundings, we don´t really matter in a sense that we would affect the course of the world in one way or the other, but we anyway keep it going. For the system we are perfect, and in the same time we are perfect examples of why representative democracy is a sorrowful farce. We don´t have the time, the means or the understanding to become familiar with the world in a way that we could make reasonable decisions about it. We are not ready for self-rule, we are barely adequate to vote.

Politicians are sold to us, besides with the illusion of intelligence that is caused by higher than average confidence that is caused by average intelligence at most, with empty slogans that appeal to our emotions but don´t really mean anything. And they don´t even keep their promises, which don´t therefore have any actual meaning anyway. With the exception of some tiny superficial details, the policies stay the same regardless of which party is in power and the party-devoted masses change their own opinions to match their party´s official line. In this circus, the ones whose turn it is to be in the opposition always offer simple solutions to complicated questions and changing the roles every four years creates an illusion of change, even though any fundamental issues are rarely even taken into discussion. Democracy has reached the same point as television and movie series that have been running for too long and have become second-hand embarrassment causing parodies of themselves.

Less than 10 percent of us trust in politicians but majority of us still vote and we take it as a civic duty. Voting is merely mental masturbation. Voting liberates us from thinking and from the responsibility of the consequences of our actions, as long as we obey the law. Even though the politicians are not even holding the real power or making decisions for the greater good, they are mainly working as foremen between the working class and their owners, and at the same time as scapegoats for us all. In a global world where global capital owns practically everything, it also decides for practically everything. If a single nation tries to make decisions against it to improve conservation of nature, social welfare or workers' rights, the consequence is going to be loss of investments, raise of interest rates of the national debt and summons to international court. This is also why all the natural recourses and profitable state-owned companies are privatized, by stripping the nations of their own income sources they are made even more dependent on the capital. Same people are smoothly changing from politics to business and back in a way that they are making decision that benefit themselves and their inner circle, or they make those decision in order to get a well-paid job as a reward after their political career.

 Our consumer habits are a way more effective way to have any kind of effect on the world than voting. This is sugar coated by talking about democratic deficit or lack of political will, but still the world doesn´t need a conspiracy of the lizard people in order to be like it is, we just haven´t evolved beyond this as a species. Or at least the lizard people are not shape shifters that physically differ from us in any way, their actions are just directed by the same primitive parts of the brain as other reptilians. They are lacking the internal dimension that would make them even apes and while guided by their distorted instinct of self-preservation, they don´t have any other option but to try and collect as much money and power as possible.

 The true conflict is not the people against the government, or at least it shouldn´t be. The government could be the greatest thing ever if it worked as it is meant to work, and the stronger the government the better. Weak government doesn´t mean more freedom and justice, it means the law of the jungle and the rule of the strongest. And seeing freedom as an absolute virtue is a consequence of an overly positive idea of man anyway. The greediest and the most vicious are always going to abuse freedoms to their own personal gain, and they are always going to win in the end, because they are the greediest and the most vicious. The ones campaigning for weaker government and smaller public sector are the ones who only want the government to secure their right to oppress the less fortunate. Individuals should have as much freedoms as possible, as long they are not hurting anyone else, but corporations, financial sector and others in power should be strictly controlled, or they are always going to use their position to grow so big that they destroy everything around them. Nothing should be allowed to grow to be too big to fall because it gives absolute freedom to do anything without the fear of consequences. Unbridled capitalism inevitably leads to fascism.

Hitler was voted to power in a free election despite telling already ten years beforehand what would follow, and he probably didn´t ever personally kill anyone. Yet we have made him the embodiment of evil, even though there is a little Hitler living in every one of us. None of us get that much done just by ourselves, not in good nor in evil. The worst serial killers have only been able to kill tens of peoples, a couple of hundred at tops. As horrible as it is, it´s nothing compared to those tens and hundreds of millions of murders by evil regimes that were carried out by ordinary people just following orders. Following orders doesn´t however take away our moral responsibilities for our actions, even if everyone else is following them as well. Hitler could have been stopped multiple times before he solidified his power, but people thinking about their own personal interests didn´t want to do it. At the latest the army should have captured the power when he was cleansing the top of it, but the remaining officers saw an opportunity for quick promotions instead. There is also living within every one of us a German military officer, who is willing to sacrifice even his honor for his ambition.

 The Israeli government has disrespected the memory of the holocaust victims by using them as an excuse for their own conquest of lebensraum. A little bit in a same way as the me-too movement has disrespected rape victims by claiming that their experiences have not been any worse than getting padded on the butt by your senile old boss who doesn´t understand that it hasn´t been socially accepted behavior since the 60s.

 When Vladimir Putin orders an ex-spy to be liquidated with radioactive polonium, it is of course a horrible crime, but also an honest message that he is not to be fucked with. Nixon tried to do the same by ordering unarmed students to be shot for protesting against the war in Vietnam, but it only led to more protests since the president of the United States is not actually in charge. That´s why the United States just locks its objectors away to be tortured without a trial or kills them with predator drones that cause so many civilian casualties, that they managed to get the children of some countries to be afraid of sunshine, since those drones attack like a lightning from the clear sky. Where FSP is allowed to blow up buildings by themselves, the CIA has to train terrorist groups for it.

 Societies are just large collections of individuals and everyone's little choices in everyday life creates the atmosphere we are living in. The political system is just the frame in which everything functions and one system doesn't necessarily have to be better than the other. Good dictatorship could be better than shitty pseudo democracy. The United States intelligent agencies didn't manage to assassinate Fidel Castro despite trying for hundreds of times but Lee Harvey Oswald shot Kennedy right under their eyes and all he needed was a little bit of magic. Child mortality rate in Cuba decreased tenfold after Castro rose to power, illiteracy and unemployment were practically rooted out, education and healthcare systems became one of the best in the world. The revolutionaries surely made some mistakes when they tried to change the country too radically without the necessary expertise and that combined with the criminal trade embargo by the United States kept them from ever reaching the western material standards of living, which on the other hand might be a good thing, considering the soulless materialism it has led to. Nevertheless, Fidel Castro was the most important head of state of the latter half of the twentieth century, where Ronald Reagan and Margaret Thatcher were the worst.

Most of us are good people. We just want to live in peace without hurting anyone, earn our living and spend time with our loved ones. But we are also greedy, inconsiderate, selfish and short-sighted. Homo Sapiens is a way better description of our egos than the actual us and the name probably contains a fair amount of irony. In the same way as The Prince by Machiavelli and The Art of Being Right by Schopenhauer were meant to fuck with us and Nineteen Eighty-Four by Orwell was meant as a warning, but we have related to all of them as instructional. Intelligence is by no means a typical attribute to us. From time to time there has happened to be born exceptional individuals whose ideas and inventions we have used to create the illusion of the wise man. But in the same time those inventions have made our lives so much easier that evolution has changed its direction and our intelligence has started to decline.

No-one is ought to be called stupid and we take it as a great insult, usually because the truth hurts. Already in school we bully those who are most eager to learn, we take too complicated reasoning as pointless excuses and we win arguments by pleading to emotions instead of reason, we attack the person instead of sticking to the facts. We laugh at people who are too honest and work for the greater good more than is customary; we see them as simple and naïve. The ones thinking outside the box and speaking the truth we see as crazy. We see getting triggered as an argument in our favor, even though it quite literally means that we go into the emotional state of an upset infant, and while our emotions should be taken into consideration, we should not be taking part in a grown-up conversation. Gracefully said we are emotional persons, that is just another way of saying we are not rational. We feel that things are in a certain way, and since our brain sees the evidence that support that experience as more believable, we all think we are smarter than average and use ourselves as the standard for everything. It is equally insane to function as others are expecting us to just to get their approval, as it is to do things our own way and get excluded because of it, and in our own experience we are just the amount of lazy, hard-working, rational, emotional, helpful, selfish, sane and insane as we ought to be, anything more or less wouldn´t be normal. We have adapted to the culture just enough, we follow the rules that are reasonable and because we understand way more than we show, we don´t believe everything that everyone else seems to believe. We all play this ridiculous game where we try to look sane, which is in itself insane, since sanity doesn´t even exist.

When we choose something, we simultaneously block out the options that are contradicting the thing that we have chosen, and we are forced to regard it as smarter than the other options or we are going to feel stupid, therefore we are suspicious or even hostile towards people who make a different choice. We think things are stupid, sometimes because we understand them, but usually because we don´t, and the more stupid we are, the harder it is for us to know that we are stupid.

We are also confusing education with intelligence, even though they don´t necessarily have to have anything to do with each other. Memorizing things doesn´t make us intelligent nor does the understanding of their rationales, a lot of times quite the opposite. Especially if we relate to knowledge as something outside of ourselves, something that we possess, without molding it as part of our personality and worldview in a way that we understand it besides in relation to everything else, but also the conditions that it requires to be either true or false, and without being able to forget it completely and then build it up again from the scratch.

The more we study something, the harder it is to accept anything that is against what we have learned, and we easily fall in love with our own truth. More important than the verbal understanding of facts, is the broadness of our perspective and the meaning we give them, since we are always going to interpret them according to our inner values. This is, beside economic interests and pursuit of other personal benefits, the biggest reason why we come to completely different conclusion based on the same facts: we interpret the world to be the way we feel and want it to be. And when we get disappointed by our truth, it feels liked getting betrayed by a loved one and we easily change from one extreme to another. From a communist into a banker or from the most passionate advocate of organic farming into its hardest critic, from vegan to paleo or the other way around, but very rarely straight to the happy medium. Instead of the amount of knowledge that we have, it´s more important to find the balance between how much we know and how much of it we can handle emotionally. If we know too much, we become distressed and get easily drifted to the extremes. If we know too little, we are in better balance and our confidence grows but we make worse decision, or at least we make them with worse reasoning.

 Music affects our subconscious straight past our conscious mind and since our taste in music shows the state of mind that we are most comfortable with, it could tell more about our true intelligence than our education or IQ, if we only knew how to interpret it. The imbeciles playing loud music in public places regardless of other people are usually listening to some mindless thumping and the sophisticated intellectuals estranged from reality go to operas. Depressed church burners listen to black metal and suburban youth taking themselves too seriously listen to gangsta rap. All of us have a little bit of all of them inside of us and usually we like many different genres, some of us even like all of them, and the same music has different effects on the different levels of consciousness. A simple pop melody can really touch an intellectual and complicated classical masterpiece raise sophisticated ideas into the mind of a manual worker. Same music can also arouse completely opposite emotions in us and there can be so many different thoughts tied to those emotions, that there are way too many variables for a scientific theory. Music can nevertheless work as a perfect tool for introspection instead, especially the kind of music that we don´t like, since it raises up emotions that we don´t want to feel.

 This is why hit songs so often are single-use products for the simple masses and contain so little deeper content that they can´t stand the test of time once they get out of fashion, a musical counterpart for Pokemon Go or the fidget spinner. Hit songs can also turn into timeless classics and sometimes depth has even been in fashion, but then the songs are often hits and classics for different reasons in a same way as good children´s movies also work for adults and sporting events are sold to the uneducated casual audiences mainly as purely emotional experiences, even on the cost of the athletic aspects.

 There is nevertheless absolutely nothing wrong with being simple and a lot of times simple people are smarter than the intellectuals who stumble over their own intelligence. Nor does intelligence automatically make anyone a good person, a lot of times quite the opposite. Many of the greatest minds of history have been really difficult personalities and most of the tyrants have been smarter than average. Since the balance between sense and sensibility is more important than the absolute amount of either one of them, a simpler person can come to exactly the same conclusions without constant overthinking and still has the time and energy to actually function in everyday life. Thinking is not actually useful unless something goes wrong. If something is not broken why fix it and so forth. But since perfectness doesn't exist, we are always in need for some smart-ass to point out the mistakes and shortcomings of our society.

 As a society we are now approximately in the same situation as a man who has been working overtime for the past couple of years with the aid of pain pills and psychiatric medication, but whose consumer credits are still constantly maxed out. There are employee co-operation negotiations starting next week and the bubble can burst at any time, and furthermore we have also just found out that we have contracted gonorrhea, but we don't know how to react to it, since we are not sure if we have gotten it from the wife or from the girlfriend.

 We look at the world from within ourselves and we see way better justifications for our own reasonable actions than for the absurdities everyone else is up to. Besides ourselves, we are interpreting the actions of our family, friends and group under the same delusion, directly in respect of our emotional attachment to them, and it's not limited only to the people we are in contact with. We create similar emotional bonds to public figures, even fictional characters and especially to athletes. We approve from our own team the exact same actions that would cause us to get furious if done by the opposition, and we even encourage them. We pay insane amounts of money for grown-ups to play different games for a living and we create an incredibly strong emotional bond to events that we have nothing to do with and that don´t actually mean anything.

 Giving meaning to things that don´t have any meaning other than the one we are giving to them, helps us to give meaning to life and makes it more than just survival, as long as we don´t give them more meaning than to survival and life itself.

 Children's playing is practice for life and it´s completely understandable, or even advisable, that also adults feel a little childish from time to time. As well as development of sportsmanship and good physical health, learning cooperation and how to handle disappointment and all the other positive and useful things that playing sports can offer to us. But we have molded them into a meaningless spectacle for promoting the sales of the merchandise. Salaries of the athletes have gotten completely out of hand and even though he is not the crazy one who asks, it directs money to an insane direction when at the same time we can´t afford to hire enough people for healthcare, education and the protection of society. One is not directly away from the other, but it still indicates where our system directs more money and what we value more. We see kicking around a ball or skating around on ice as so much more important than saving a life that it´s paid ten or even hundredfold more.

In hockey there have even been whole seasons skipped when millionaires and billionaires have been fighting over money. In football there are girly men diving on the fields while hooligans are fighting in the stands and players and referees have even been killed when emotions have sparked over worse than with a bunch of 3-year-olds fighting in a sandpit. There are the construction and maintenance costs of the oversized arenas, building of the Olympic villages and motorsports encouraging for the overuse of fossil fuels. Top athletes are also artificially multiplying their need for energy, that could be considered quite questionable when at the same time a large portion of the people of the world are suffering for malnutrition and food production is overloading the environment in a way that animals and plants are getting extinct and ecosystems destroyed as we are clearing land for agriculture. Doping is so commonly used that it´s probably impossible to be successful without it in any discipline that is based on physical performance, testing in professional sports is a joke and the results of the Olympics are still being corrected ten years after the original medals were given.

Officially banning performance enhancing substances is also causing the clean athletes to be in emotionally unfair situation if they know, or at least believe to know, that all of their fellow competitors are using something, and begin to doubt their own chances as a result. And the ones using doping are going to have to live the rest of their lives with the knowledge that their accomplishments mean absolutely nothing. Surely, they have managed to cheat appreciation and possibly quite large economic benefit for themselves, and the use of banned substances doesn´t mean that they didn´t have to work just as hard or possibly even harder than everyone else. But regardles of how sure they are about everyone else cheating as well, they have offended good sportsmanship and nullified the only thing that really mattered. All sports are essentially about competing within made up but clearly defined rules and if we try to bend those rules, we might as well participate in Le Tour de France with a motorcycle.

 At the top, the difference between greatness and mediocrity is so small that it´s not only a question of who is using doping and who is not, but who is the best at using it. If we would allow the use of absolutely everything and reward also the doctors beside the athletes, we wouldn´t have to waste money and resources for testing and covering up the use, possibly in ways that are harmful to the athletes and hinder their optimal performance. Instead of taking the highest doses on the training season, the athletes could be juiced to the gills and at their absolute peak at the exactly right time and the audiences would get to enjoy the greatest performances possible. By studying the effects of the different substances and extreme physical and mental stress, we could also possibly learn something useful that could be adapted to other medicine and competitive sports at the highest level could justify their existence in the same way as space research. An athlete never sees a healthy day and by monitoring them close enough, that can never be achieved with traditional questionnaire surveys, we could possibly learn something about the birth mechanisms of different illnesses instead of just treating their symptoms with different medications.

Even our health has been commercialized and our attitude towards it has developed ridiculous features. We drive to the gym with a car, to walk on a treadmill in tactical, technical and foremost fashionable tights and we buy all our nutrients in their own separate jars, from which we then assemble a meal that is as convenient as Ikea furniture. We have been sold the myth of optimal fitness as promotive of health, even though too hard training merely wears out the body, stressing over food turns over its health benefits and top athletes also suffer from depression manifold compared to the average population.

Some of us exercise regularly and eat downright neurotically healthy but fall ill anyway. Some of us eat and do only whatever comes to mind, don't worry about anything and stay in perfect health despite an unhealthy way of life. The rest of us are somewhere in between and what happens to us seems to almost depend on mere luck. If we were able to understand all the different sides and how they are working together, we could probably improve our wellbeing with relatively small changes.

With many diseases we know that a healthy diet and moderate exercise would, besides preventing diseases, also ease the symptoms of diseases that we already have, but we much rather cover their symptoms with different medications that we eat, besides for the diseases, even for their potential risk factors. In addition, we eat a shitload of white sugar, refined flower, Pop Tarts, Corn Dogs, Cheese Puffs and Sautéed Racoons´ Assholes on a stick, along with a fuckton of other convenience foods that are all filled with the same offal that is driven through a meatgrinder and then chemically colored and spiced. In our defense, we are manipulated into doing so by professional fabulists, sugar is hidden in almost everything, body positive people see information about health problems caused by overweight as fat shaming and junk food is so much cheaper, that by eating like this we save just enough money to afford our meds.

It´s so much easier for us to add a couple off pills a day, than to give up anything, that instead of pursuing overall wellbeing, we are willing to also accept the side-effects that every drug causes. Even though side-effect is a misleading term since they don´t really exist, only different effects of which some are more, and some are less wanted. Different chemicals cause different changes in the body, some of which mechanisms we don´t even understand, but pharmaceutical industry has anyway got us convinced that they are always good for us, whatever inconvenience we may have. Partly by downright lying and lawlessness, that has caused them billions of dollars in fines, but is nothing compared to their profits. Pharmaceutical industry is also the biggest lobbyist trying to keep cannabis illegal. The medical benefits of cannabis have been known for thousands of years and it is still a safer and more effective medication to many conditions than any modern drug, but since it can´t be patented, pharmaceutical companies, and the doctors educated and influenced by them, downplay its benefits despite research and experiences of the patients. And at the same time, they are trying to copy its effects with synthetic versions, that have turned out to be both ineffective and extremely dangerous.

The pharmaceutical industry has also partly ruined the good reputation of medicine, even though the latter´s accomplishments have saved millions of lives and greatly improved our wellbeing. The main function of the pharmaceutical industry is to produce profit and it has led to, besides the fabrication of research results, corruption of the facets giving recommendations for treatments and approving drugs for sale, overuse of drugs, that has turned out to have horrible consequences especially with antibiotics, and many more questionable things, also to that many of us don´t believe in anything that western medicine has to offer anymore. We leave our children unvaccinated and try to treat cancer with homeopathy and angel therapy because we feel betrayed by the one facet that should be only concerned about our wellbeing.

By nationalizing pharmaceutical companies, turning them into nonprofit corporations and holding people personally responsible, instead of fining the companies, when they get caught breaking the law, we could make the pharmaceutical industry serve healthcare instead of healthcare serving the pharmaceutical industry. If a drug gets approved for sale by conscious manipulation of the research results, every person it kills or harms should be considered a homicide or an assault and the people responsible should be sentenced according to it. We could still develop better drugs and reward the researchers with big bonuses for breakthroughs, but the drugs wouldn´t have to be modified just because of patents going old. The education of the doctors and recommendations for treatments could be designed only from the point of view of benefiting the patients and lifestyle changes combined with more gentle treatments could be recommended as the first option in all non-acute situations.

In addition to drugs having injurious effect on the users, and a lot of times in vain when they are taken just for potential risk factors or the ratio between benefits and side-effects is so poor that we are practically just changing a disease for another, that can then be treated with other drugs, the mass production of them in the developing countries causes environmental hazards and health problems to the local populations due to toxic waste and chemical pollution. Those chemicals are also spread into the environment with human excrement and they end up as part of the food chain, as do other environmental toxins, and hormones and antibiotics from meat production. Little by little our environment becomes more and more harmful and causes more diseases, for which we eat and produce even more drugs.

Our environment has changed so drastically in such a short time that its effect to our health is impossible to understand. The combined effect of different drugs, toxins, plastics, radiations and energy fields, additives and building materials and so on can be absolutely anything. Intelligent animals are not supposed to shit in their own nests, but we have pushed the whole planet on the brink of destruction in the short time that it has been technologically possible. All civilizations have collapsed on their own impossibilities, building of phallic symbols and temples, and the general wasting of resources in order to compensate for our feelings of nothingness and inadequacy. In the global world the threats have also become global and are even threatening our survival as a species.

Globalization has always, and still is, based on exploitation and pillaging the less developed countries. From the great expeditions, East India Company and the Opium wars, it has always been about the same thing; we have felt that we are entitled to other countries' riches and depending on the situation we have either directly conquered them or bribed their corrupted leaders. We are still cooperating with corrupted governments, selling weapons to countries that are constantly committing crimes against humanity and organizing revolutions in countries whose leaders are trying to use their natural resources to benefit their own people.

Instead of letting those countries develop in peace, we are using them to spread disorder around the world and we use the refugee crisis to create confrontation between people in order to make them easier to control. The war on terror is a never-ending self-feeding process that is replacing the war on drugs, because war is not only an economical, but also a psychological necessity. And it´s not only creating conflict between the original populations and the immigrant populations against each other, but also within those populations in a way that instead of understanding and respecting each other, the different cultures are molded into pulp that is not satisfying anyone and instead of unity we have global civil war. That war is not completely open, but it is enough to keep people so suspicious towards each other that it is easy for them to be controlled by the corporate fascistic government of the new world order.

Nor does that government, like any other government, have any other real plans but to stay in power. Money allows us to control everything and by controlling money we control everything else as well. We don´t have any kind direction or masterplan. There is no conspiracy by the elites to control the world and direct it to a certain direction, there is just a bunch of people who want to get the biggest possible piece of the pie, and who are doing it quite openly.

After securing our basic needs, there are only things that we are using to pass the time and amuse ourselves. With the amount of money and resources that we are spending on entertainment, we could cover the basic needs for everyone, stabilize the world and figure out together where we are going. This was achieved even by a group of apes whose alpha males happened to all die at the same time and they didn't allow anyone to get in power by themselves anymore. After that, the stress hormone levels of all the individuals lowered and the group was doing much better as a whole. We are however constantly using more and more resources for entertainment, in order to distract ourselves from the injustices of the world. But there are no private actions anymore in the global world, everything we do affects everything else and everything we spend is taken away from someone else, even if it's from the other side of the world or from the future generations.

At the same time as we are pondering how to make our resources last, we are still measuring our success with GDP, the amount that we are spending and producing. The tiny little changes we are doing to give our economy artificial respiration, are in a long run as useful as taking care of drug addiction by counterfeiting prescriptions. We see constant growth and development as measures of success, even though the only thing beside us that grows and develops just for the sake of it is cancer. Crocodiles haven't changed for hundreds of millions of years and they are doing just fine, and they are probably going to keep on living for a long time after we have managed to kill ourselves with our constant rush. We don´t have any kind of idea about where we are going, but we are nevertheless trying to get there as fast as possible. Kind of in a same way that we are happy when time just flies, even though there is a very limited amount of it for every single one of us. As boring and distressing it may be, it might be a good idea for us to just sit down for a moment and do absolutely nothing.

We are trying to solve our problems by doing more work, but work doesn´t have any kind of intrinsic value. A large portion of what we do is already useless and even harmful. We are constantly developing and producing new throw away products and using advertising to fabricate an illusion of them being needed, we build artificial paradises in the desert and have turned the whole world into a shopping mall. Earth Overshoot Day sounds like something we celebrate every day, but it´s actually the day when we have used our renewable resources for that year and the date gets earlier every year. And yet we relate to environmentalists with mocking and even hostility because they haven´t understood that actually doing something about those things cause inconvenience in our everyday lives. Instead of seeing ourselves as an inseparable part of nature, that we can´t survive without, we see nature just as a commodity that we can exploit as much as we please. The only allowed action for the environment is to fly to a conference with a private plane to sign uncommitted deals and then to pose for the cameras as if everything was taken care of.

We have changed the world so much in the last two centuries that we have been imprisoned by our own progress. We can't just jump back to the time when we were in balance with the nature because the result would be approximately the same standard of living as before the industrial revolution, divided with population growth since then. But we have also created enormous problems that can escalate either one at a time or all together, starting a chain reaction that causes our environment to become inhabitable. Deforestation, overfishing, climate change and disappearance of biodiversity, artificial intelligence going nuts, nuclear weapons, collapse of the economic system, fossil fuels running out, contamination of the environment, fresh water running out, soil fertility decline and overpopulation, which is not even a problem compared to the overload to the environment caused by our standard of living, are all threats that we don't have any real solutions for.

There is 5 percent of the world's population living in the United States, but they are spending 25 percent of the resources. And to those countries, who for some reason don't want to voluntarily imitate the culture that has produced hundreds of school shootings, millions of homeless people, the world's biggest prison population working as slave labor, as well as education and healthcare systems that are considered a joke, the world's greatest rogue state brings its gospel of pseudo democracy, corporate fascism and overconsumption by force. The roots of the world police are by all means in freedom, but in a very special kind of freedom that

rich white slave owners declared to consider mainly themselves. And that's the reason they wanted the right to bear
arms, so that any government thinking about the common
good would never try to limit their right to own land and
people.

 We spend billions of dollars a year for commercials targeted
directly to children, in order to get them to connect happiness with materialism as early as possible. The investment
pays itself back manifold when we turn from citizens into
consumers and spend the rest of our lives trying to relive the
experience of finally getting the toy that we so desperately
wanted. By drowning our children into presents every
Christmas, we are peeing into the cereals of the future generations in so many ways that it could be better if we did so
literally. Besides giving them an overdose of presents, that
leaves emotional memory that can later be insurmountable,
the value of a single present stays so little that half of them
are broken or lose their meaning before the holidays are
over. And once they get hooked on stuff, they'll never get
unhooked, nor get more than momentary satisfaction from
it, but they nevertheless pass that desire on to the next generation, somehow imagining that it could make them happy.

Everything around us feeds that desire, everything has been
commercialized, every place is full of commercials, television and social media are constantly showing us people who
have everything we want and who we would want to be

alike, even though those people are not even real. But we are not necessarily doing it on purpose, it´s just how our brain was programmed to function when we were still living in small groups in similar surroundings and doing worse than someone else meant we were probably doing something wrong.

 We mimic their style and buy all kind of unnecessary things in order to stay fashionable, even though all fashion phenomenons have always looked equally ridiculous. Following fashion and seeing things stylish just because everyone else sees them that way is one of the best examples of how we give up ourselves in order to be part of the herd. Laughing at someone for not following fashion is slave´s laughter to another for giving up their chains. A lot of times there is also a similar thing related to fashion, as with those animals who have developed attributes that are unfavorable for survival and demonstrate their suitability for mating by surviving regardless of those attributes. This can be seen among other things in keeping our lower backs, knees or ankles bare during winter, in order to prove that we are not afraid of urinary tract infection; since we usually ape people who are famous for one attribute or skill at most, and that is very rarely their intelligence.

We wait for weeks to get to a fancy restaurant and pay an arm and a leg for a serving the size of flyshit when there is a child starving to death in every six seconds. We pay hundreds of millions for a painting whose painter died poor and forgotten. Even though our sense of taste changes in few weeks according to what we eat, and beauty is always in the eye of the beholder. Wine tasters choose the cheapest wine as long as it is in the most expensive bottle and art critics were praising paintings that were, in fact, painted by a chimpanzee.

We are in constant need for new toys, bigger televisions, fancier cars, more exotic holidays and more of everything. We also somehow imagine that we have deserved them, and even if we don´t, things are designed to break down and in digital age they just stop being updated so we are anyway going to have to replace them. All this so-called progress is, however, superficial and meaningless. It doesn´t matter how those new toys are. Only how our experiences of them are. When the first Nintendo came out, it was at least as great of an experience as the new super consoles with their sharper than reality graphics and the story or the feeling of a movie doesn´t get any better with special effects and bigger screen. The greatest virtual reality doesn´t match going out and really seeing the world. In essence everything is just about us using different kind of stimulations to create an experience inside our heads. And as a consequence of all the superfluous technology, that experience seems to rather have flattened and we take everything for granted. When we get used to something newer and fancier, we don´t want to ever go back and now we are also used to newer and fancier coming faster all the time. We are severely addicted to smart drugs. But the little inventions and applications that are making life easier are not necessarily making it any better. They are just leaving out the experiences we got from doing things by ourselves and we have to replace them with something artificial. And at the same time, they are leaving out the lessons we got from either succeeding or failing in them.

We know that overconsumption and pollution are problems but at the same time our culture encourages us to consume and the impact of one person is so small that we don't feel like our actions matter if everybody else is not changing their behavior as well, and precisely those things that we want are actually really needed. Our phone has to be renewed every year because the last one's camera had only one hundred million megapixels, our neighbor bought a new car as well and it is impossible to see anything out of a TV that is not at least sixty inches big and curved. After fulfilling our basic needs, the relation between wealth and happiness is depending on what everyone else has. We estimate the amount of income, where either increasing or decreasing it lowers our happiness, very differently depending on how rich the environment we are living in is.

Besides that, we can't all just move back into the wild and start living in balance with the nature, since there is way too many of us for that, it's also meaningless in the big picture, because the effect of one person is so small. If our actions in our whole lifetime would postpone the apocalypse for just one second, that would already mean over 200 years if everyone else also did the same. But if we give up more than we can, suffer because of it and make ourselves martyrs, we are not encouraging anyone to follow our lead, and especially if we try to force our choices upon people, we cause counter reaction and indirectly increase the overall load. We have even adjusted our cars to pollute as much as possible, because we hate the emission standards. Or increased our meat consumption because we hate vegans, and smoking because we hate it's unhealthiness. We are really interesting in that way.

 Even though a plant-based diet is clearly better, at least for the animals and for the environment, going on a plant-based diet doesn't make us better than anyone else. If we feel in our heart that eating animals is wrong and stop doing so, we are better compared to our former selves in a sense that we changed our actions because we felt it was the right thing to do, but we are in no way, shape or form better than someone who feels that they need to eat meat in order to survive and acts according to that feeling. Even if there wasn't any essential nutrients in meat that we couldn't get from plants and supplements, believing there was would cause psycho-somatic symptoms if we were forced to stop eating meat and even if we were forcing ourselves into doing so. And if that belief was deep enough, it could even stop our bodies from converting vitamin A and omega 3 fatty acids into the right form for us. Only when our bodies and minds are in perfect balance, can they really work optimally, but even then, only within the limitations of their actual biological structures. No matter how enlightened we may be, we are not able to live on just sunlight and water.

 By giving up something we don´t really need, we are freeing ourselves from the slavery of materialism and increasing our happiness. And we don´t need to make major changes at once, since we are only one of seven billion people and we are not solely responsible for saving the world. Doing the right thing and pursuing happiness doesn´t have to be contradictory, they go hand in hand once we get in balance. Dismissing good deeds because they are also making us feel good about ourselves or seeing the self-satisfaction that we get for doing the right thing somehow as a bad thing is just a consequence of us still being emotionally on a level of a defiant aged child.

 It is easy for us to hate Hitler and others like him, of whom we have made the embodiment of evil, and on the other hand look up to saints since they are so far from us that they feel almost like abstractions. But in those who are close to us, it´s easier for us to tolerate imperfection than perfection. We don´t change our own behavior because we can´t emotionally handle the consequences of it. We are not going to hell because we believe in it, but because we don´t.

When we are doing the right thing, the happiness stemming from inside of us increases and we need less external pleasures. We can work less and spend more time with our loved ones. We can also spread work more evenly, since the improvement of technology makes sure that there is not going to be enough of it for everyone anyway, especially if we stop buying and producing so much useless and excessive stuff. And when all the others are following our example, our brain stops getting jealous of everything they own and little by little we can change the course of our evolution. Instead of materialism, we focus on our emotional and spiritual well-being, cooperation instead of competition, the society supports our evolution and we support the evolution of society. Nature gets to heal itself and we all live in perfect harmony.

Although we still fly from time to time to a tourist attraction to get drunk for a week, even if one flight would double our carbon footprint, since travelling expands the mind, even if we just went there to relax in holiday feelings while the locals actually have to work for a living. Tripping on our own couch by eating mushrooms would expand our minds way more though, since it would allow us to see our own culture from the outside, instead of going out and wondering about the superficial differences of foreign cultures as if visiting a zoo.

This is the reason why psychedelics are so strictly forbidden and dangerous for the system, they help us free ourselves from our cultural programming. On the contrary, alcohol helps us free ourselves from thinking and is therefore the perfect slave drug. Getting drunk works as a blow-off valve that never allows us to build up enough pressure for real change. Besides alcohol, we are only allowed, and sometimes pressured, to use drugs that make profit for the Big Pharma and are meant to keep us productive and obedient. Drug use as an offence is merely a thoughtcrime. Apart from heroin, crystal meth and a couple others of the worst poisons, most drugs are less harmful than alcohol and by choosing them, we show that we are not willing to just blindly follow orders. All the hard drugs are also inventions of the pharmaceutical industry and were originally marketed to us as completely safe, and they are still fed to us just a little bit modified in such quantities that there is way more people dying for prescription drugs than illegal drugs. Any drugs are probably not good for us, at least when used regularly, but apart from ourselves, drug use is completely victimless and it being a crime is absurd, considering what should be the fundamental purpose of laws.

In every culture people have felt the need to occasionally change their level of consciousness in one way or another and it is a crime against humanity to allow only the use of one of the most harmful and least useful substances for that purpose. Nor did even the prohibition of alcohol work in any way, since that need is so powerful that even animals do it. Moose eat fermented apples and wreak havoc while drunk, whereas dolphins who are known for their intellect are composedly tripping with pufferfish poison, reindeers are eating magic mushrooms and kangaroos are doing opium.

Prohibition created the base for organized crime, changed alcohol culture more to binge drinking and ate away people´s respect for law. Still the same people who are firmly against illegal drugs say that they would smuggle alcohol if it was to be prohibited. If booze is not enough, is anything?

The war against drugs brought about cartels and an insane amount of violence, made drug addicts criminals and shut a large group of people out of society, possibly just because of one little mistake that they made when they were young. Prohibition also brought about an unhealthy attitude and increased drug abuse the same way it did with alcohol. Drug education that is based on lies and exaggeration creates a strict counter reaction that makes it considerably harder to relate to drugs rationally. There is the excitement of being an outlaw associated with drug use and it is seen as a civic right that is only maintained by using every day. In addition, the use is driving us to seek the company of other users, where the drug favorable attitudes are feeding each other and real conversations with people with different kind of values may be left out completely.

We drift towards illegal drugs much easier if we have some kind of problems already and we meet other problematic people in a social environment where the usage of different substances is encouraged and hard drugs are readily available. And still the percentage of people getting addicted is not any higher with those who are experimenting with illegal drugs as compared to those drinking alcohol, and most people quit or at least cut down their drug use around their 30s. Some of us blame drugs for all of our problems once we get sober, but if we felt the need to use them previously, but don´t feel that need anymore, after using them, they clearly had some kind of role in that growth process. If we would include all psychoactive substances into public conversation and related to them rationally without moralizing, or over-reactions to the other direction, they could be part of the whole humanity´s growth process instead of being an enormous problem.

Many artists, trailblazers of science and other extraordinary people have used different substances in order to expand their minds or to be able to deal with their expanded minds. There is very rarely anything new created by mediocrity and the inner conflicts where genius is upwelled from can be very hard to deal with, especially if we have to function in the world where very few people are functioning on that same level of consciousness. Drugs don´t bring anything from the outside, but they can be useful tools that help us to fulfill our potential. As long as we know how to give them up once they are no longer serving their purpose.

One of the best qualities of alcohol is that it is such a bad drug. It can get us more fucked up than any other substance and it causes hangover, so it´s not that easy to use in every-day life. Many of the other substances increase our function-ality in the beginning and they are mostly affecting our mood, so from the outside we seem to be more or less so-ber. Problems creep along imperceptibly and when we be-come aware of them, it can be already too late to let go. And the better the drugs feel in the beginning, the easier and the more insidiously the addiction can be born, and the higher the price that we are going to have to pay for them in the end gets.

Besides therapeutic use, different substances could also be useful in different rituals and social events, where those ex-periences would be more important than the substances themselves and their purpose would be to help us get more in balance with ourselves, so our need for using them would decrease. Excessive use and bad trips can really fuck us up for a long time and prolonged sobriety is pretty much the only way for truly finding ourselves. Even Terence McKenna hung up the phone eventually. But although psychedelics don´t lead to enlightenment, since we have to anyway inter-pret the experiences in our everyday state of mind, they can nevertheless teach us a lot about ourselves. Spending one night in introspection under the influence of magic mush-rooms would in many ways seem like a better rite of passage than the current one, where we spent ten years binge drink-ing and having casual sex.

Then the production of drugs could also be ecologically sustainable. At the moment the manufacturing of different substances is burdening the environment in a way that only growing them on our own yard or picking them from the nature can be seen as a purely personal matter. There are forests cut and land taken away from food production in order to grow Cannabis, Coca and Opium and the toxic chemicals used in the manufacturing of synthetic drugs are poisoning the environment. Coffee and tobacco are also drugs, whose farming requires a lot of resources and they are usually used daily, since they are not really perceived as drugs, because we have such high tolerance for them as a consequence of that daily use.

Cigarettes are in many ways a prime example of everything that is wrong with the world. A product of an evil corporation that is both useless and harmful to its user, that has been sunk so deep into the culture by emotional advertising, that even the people who have been born after that advertising has already ended will fight until the bitter end for their right to sacrifice their money and health to it. Primary production is run by child and slave labor or at least slave-like wages and the employees are suffering from health hazards since nicotine is absorbed so efficiently through the skin. There is huge amounts of water and other resources wasted into farming and hundreds of poisonous chemicals are added to cigarettes in order to make them even more addicting.

If we continue in the same way that we have thus far, there is a realistic possibility that we are not going to survive as a species even until the sun shuts down or some other event that is out of our hands makes life on earth impossible. Even if we didn't believe in the man-made climate change, nuclear winter or artificial intelligence and the revolution of the machines, there are multiple other risks, some of which we haven't even begun to understand as of yet, that could at their worst lead to an unstoppable chain reaction. Even some of the world's leading intellectuals see this as so probable that they see conquering space and moving to another planet as our only chance for survival. That is a sign of such despair that it could also be a time for us who are not so smart to just stop for a while and think about where we are going. Not into the space anyway. The conquering of space is just a fairy tale that is meant to give us hope, but in the same time it gives us a dangerous signal that we don't really have to change anything.

We haven't managed to make it even on this planet that has so perfect conditions for life that it was practically born out of nothing and now we should somehow be able to move to a dead planet and get it to flourish. There is no point in even dreaming about moving outside of our own solar system, all the exoplanets are so far away that we should somehow be able to move faster than light, and nothing bigger than a thought is capable of doing so. And even if we found some way to conquer space and to survive forever, we would just destroy the whole universe one planet at a time. We are however tied to three dimensions, forward passing time and to this reality, where we are all going to die on this planet, apart from the three unlucky cosmonauts who died on Sojuz 11 and Elon Musk, who wants to die on Mars.

We live on a desert island that just happens to be a big rock flying through space. We are going to have to get by with the resources that we have and try to get them to last as long as possible. So far, we have been doing an equally good job as the early habitants of the Easter Islands. We are using seashells as currency and we have given only for a couple of people the permission to collect them. They are lending them for interest and the only way for us to pay back our debt is to get them from somebody else, who has taken an even bigger loan. The people that are hanging out on the beach see the ocean as a god and they are at war with the people who are living in the inland and worship the spring that they have found in the forest. They fight brutal battles in order to get fish or fresh water. The children and the less fortunate have no means to stand up for themselves, so they are spending their days collecting fruits and firewood and get to keep a tiny fraction of them for themselves. The strongest males are working out daily to stay the strongest and they oppress the others, keeping most of the food and other resources in order to keep the others too weak to revolt against them. There are statues and temples built in their honor. Once the resources start running low, we step it up a notch, so we get to use them all before they run out.

We are all going to die and one day also the last one of us. It would be really sad, but also quite ironic, if we would die as a consequence of our own actions after we have first extinguished so many other species. It's unlikely that the last person would be aware of being the last one, he would probably be some crazy recluse who would live for tens of years enjoying his own peace. For him the existence or non-existence of the rest of us would mean absolutely nothing.

Even though it's quite unlikely that we would get our resources to last forever, it would be highly unethical for us not to even try. Besides being able to guarantee humane conditions for all the already existing people, we could possibly survive for tens, hundreds or thousands of generations. In that time, we could possibly find answers to most of our problems, at least we would exist, live and experience things. And that's what it's all about. The meaning of life is a trick question, because life is its own meaning. Our life doesn't lose its significance just because we are going to die one day. There is no great goal that we should achieve as individuals or as a species. We are just existing and non-existing, in a never-ending cycle without a beginning or an end.

Infinity is twisted endlessly around itself in a way that the universe is inside of every particle that it is formed of. There is not enough energy in the whole universe for us to get our hands on the smallest possible and new reality expands in the beginning exponentially in a way that we can never reach its outer limits. But there is still a border somewhere, where the infinitely big turns into infinitely small in a same way as infinite number turns into zero if we add number one to it. On that border time and space, as we understand them, completely lose their meaning. Zero-point isn´t however located in any single point, but everywhere, since we are always in the center of the universe, regardless of where we are. The continuously expanding universe is not expanding in relation to the universes surrounding it, nor does the particle that, from our point of view, is existing only for a fraction of a second, destroy also us while it vanishes, even though we are inside of it.

Everything is constantly pulsating in their own beat between existence and non-existence. When we get into small enough particles, they seem to be both, and also everywhere, at the same time. As they are. They are found with the highest probability from where we are looking for them because we are looking for them from there. The universe seems almost infinite and eternal and everything else in between like something in between, even though their cycles are not as clear as the ones of those two opposites that are in reality the different sides of the same thing. Universe keeps expanding until it can´t keep it together anymore and collapses into itself, and then comes out from the other side of singularity and starts expanding again.

Different realities contain every potential past and future and everything that has ever happened or is ever going to happen is constantly happening everywhere, even though we are only experiencing one forward-going reality at a time. Every time we make a choice, an alternative reality in which we chose differently is created, and there are an infinite number of those realities. Every particle contains a universe whose every particle contains a universe whose every particle contains a universe, endlessly around and around in a way that every possible reality is coexisting and the one that is real depends solely on the experiencer. Mathematically thinking those realities are strings vibrating on infinite different frequencies and there is an infinite amount of those strings. The realities that are not existing, we see as dark matter and particles appear in a vacuum because it´s a vacuum only from our point of view. Emptiness is full of itself.

If we are able to overcome man, we simultaneously sentence ourselves into solitude. In our own reality we are completely alone. Everyone else is just our idea of them, in a same way that we don´t really exist in their reality. We can however at times get so close to each other, that our realities are combined, and we almost feel like the same person. We are on a level where we see everything the same way and forget ourselves completely.

When we figure out new things, we go into realities where they are real. We invent a new idea and suddenly we see it everywhere. Possibly in a way that we had never heard of it before but now we realize that it has been common knowledge for ages. This is how we have invented similar things around the world without being in touch with each other.

From time to time there can appear bugs between the different realities. We have lived in realities where Nelson Mandela has died in multiple different ways, we have spoken different languages, been brilliant mathematicians or known how to play the piano and now we are suddenly back here, without any idea of where those memories and abilities came from. We can also remember our past lives, that are however someone else´s lives, since we are living now and not then. We have always lived now, even though we have also already died as a consequence of our choices in some realities and we are only alive in those where we haven´t. Deja vu on the other hand is a legitimate memory from some previous time when we have existed.

Some of us have died and then been resurrected but that resurrection completely changes the experience of death since our conscious mind creates its own interpretation of it. Neither does the experience of timelessness exist, nor can it exist, if we have experienced something after death.

Our experience of forward-moving time is completely subjective and when there is no experiencer there is no time either. From the outside the moment of death is immeasurably short and from our perspective it is simultaneously infinitely long. Our earthly body vanishes, the sun goes out and the universe collapses just to be born again. Time starts from the beginning and repeats yet another cycle until we are born after 13,8 billion years just to die again, but our experience of the previous time we died is still continuing in the same stagnant moment. We live forever and die endlessly into the same death.

In the moment of death, we understand everything that is possible and impossible and from our perspective that moment lasts forever since there is nothing that follows it. We become one with the pure consciousness and at the same time we separate from it completely. Man and God, the condemned and the judge. We see ourselves absolutely honestly, all our good and evil deeds, our ultimate motives, everything we are proud of and all of our regrets. No more security brought about by wealth, rationalizations and cynicism. No chance to change anything or lie to ourselves anymore, everything is done and there are no more excuses. So passes the glory of the world. Unjust stays unjust, filthy stays filthy and righteous stays righteous. And it is harder for a rich man to enter the kingdom of god, than for a camel to go through the eye of a needle, unless he has turned and become like the children. We shall remember every moment as they actually were, we see the consequences of our own actions, both in good and in bad and we experience them in wordless understanding that includes everything that ever was, both in the past and in the future. This is, at the latest, when we finally really look into the mirror and create our own heaven or hell.

This book was born as therapy for the writer and it´s not meant to be taken dead seriously. All the quotes and references, both intentional and unintentional, are meant as tributes to their original authors.